Mount Athos: The History of the  and the Center of Eastern
Orthodox Monasticism

By Charles River Editors

David Profter's picture of Mount Athos

About Charles River Editors

Charles River Editors is a boutique digital publishing company, specializing in bringing history back to life with educational and engaging books on a wide range of topics. Keep up to date with our new and free offerings with this 5 second sign up on our weekly mailing list, and visit Our Kindle Author Page to see other recently published Kindle titles.

We make these books for you and always want to know our readers' opinions, so we encourage you to leave reviews and look forward to publishing new and exciting titles each week.

Introduction

A picture of the area around Vatopedi monastery

Mount Athos

"Clear water where evergreens, azaleas cool ceremoniously...a kele lost among cedars, its roof open to eagles, door unhinged...silver leaves like a congregation of spiders..." When one hears these enchanting descriptions, from poet David Posner's 1964 composition "Mount Athos," it is not difficult to understand why this sleepy paradise is often extolled as the most peaceful and private corner of Greece, if not all of Europe. Mount Athos is the easternmost finger of the Halkidiki peninsula – a mountainous sliver of land that stretches about 37.3 miles long and 4.3-7.5 miles wide, with a surface area of about 150 square miles. Towering over the tightly-packed chestnut forests and the blue, crystalline waters of the Aegean Sea at a height of 6,670 feet is the snow-dusted crest of the mighty mountain itself.

Known to the locals as *Agion Oros*, or the "Holy Mountain," the peninsula today is most famed for its exclusivity, a place that continues to bar all women and their daughters from entry. The fortress-like monasteries scattered amongst the slopes and the clusters of cells clinging to the cliffs are occupied by monks of the Eastern Orthodox Church. Of course, its male-only population is just one aspect of the peninsula's anomalous nature.

Planted on the peninsula's coast is a black Byzantine Cross, a flat, cross-shaped monument with a trinity of flared, wide-armed, Greek crosses in place of its arms and a traditional Christian cross in its center, kissed with rust. It serves as an emblem of the monastic society that resides there, and it delineates the boundary between Mount Athos and the rest of Greece. Entering this hallowed peninsula is like setting foot into a living time capsule, because life here has not changed in well over 1,000 years. Mount Athos is one of only two places on earth (the other being the Mar Saba) that chooses to run on "Byzantine time," meaning Hour 0:00:00 only begins at sundown. Moreover, it is the only territory in the world that flies the Byzantine flag, a regal, sword and cross clutching double-headed eagle set against a rippling canvas of gold.

Of course, to reduce Mount Athos to an antediluvian, single-sex monastic retreat would be an oversimplification of the fascinating history and simple, yet complex culture that has developed on this stunning strip of land. This is a place as mystically mysterious as it is serene, a space abound with treasures, miracles, and spiritual revelations. But for a place where purity and God-fearing devotion apparently reign supreme, it is certainly burdened with its fair share of controversy.

Mount Athos: The History of the Greek Mountain and the Center of Eastern Orthodox Monasticism looks at the unique region and what life has been like there since medieval times. Along with pictures depicting important people, places, and events, you will learn about Mount Athos like never before.

Mount Athos: The History of the Greek Mountain and the Center of Eastern Orthodox Monasticism

About Charles River Editors

Introduction

  Ancient History

  The Byzantine Era

  Endless Battles

  Fascinating Friars

  The Modern Era

  Online Resources

  Bibliography

Free Books by Charles River Editors

Discounted Books by Charles River Editors

Ancient History

"The man who follows Christ in solitary mourning is greater than he who praises Christ amid the congregation of men." – attributed to St. Isaac the Syrian

Fittingly, Mount Athos has long been considered by nearby residents, well before it was dominated by the Christian faith. Prior to the birth of Christianity itself, the peninsula was known as "Akte." It was only after the fateful episode starring the Thracian *gigante* Athos, as local legend dictates, that this formerly flat countryside was given its name.

Once upon a time, a terrible brawl erupted between the Thracian Giants and the Olympians, the former led by Athos, and the latter headed by Poseidon, god of the sea. In the midst of the tussle, Athos hoisted an enormous hunk of rock (soon to be the peak of Mount Athos) and flung it at Poseidon, but the mass narrowly missed its target and crashed into the sea, eventually forming the grand mountain seen today.

A conflicting version of this tale credits Poseidon for being responsible. In this account, it was the sea god who lobbed the hunk of rock at Athos. Unfortunately for Athos, Poseidon was evidently the better shot, for the peak landed atop his opponent, burying him alive. Over time, his remains were incorporated into the mountain that rose over him.

Yet another ancient myth is often associated with the etymology of the peninsula's port. Local lore has it that Apollo, the Olympian god of the sun, verse, and music (amongst many others), was struck by the golden arrow of Eros (Cupid) as retaliation for having mocked the god of love. Immediately, Apollo was imbued with a deep lust for a Naiad Nymph named Daphne. Eros then drew a lead arrow and struck Daphne, instilling her with a seething hatred for Apollo. Daphne made clear her revulsion towards him, but the lovesick Apollo remained undeterred and continued to pursue her. In an effort to escape the harassment, Daphne fled to the port of Mount Athos and remained there for some time. The port of Mount Athos was then christened "Daphne," as it continues to be known today.

Edal Anton Lefterov's picture of Daphne

The blessed – or, as some would say, cursed – pinnacle of Mount Athos was also a setting frequently referenced by fabled wordsmiths in ancient Greece. Homer and Aeschylus, the "Father of Tragedy," described the summit as the former residence of Zeus and Apollo prior to their relocation to Mount Olympus. The peninsula's peak has also been credited with hastening victories of multiple battles. For one, a great bonfire ignited on the crest of the mountain supposedly served as a beacon that led to the capture of Troy.

Shortly after Zeus and Apollo moved to Mount Olympus, a total of five cities cropped up on the Athos peninsula, where they flourished until the 3rd century BCE. These communities coexisted in harmony for several centuries, fostering their own distinct customs and trading with and alongside one another with little friction. These were built on the summit and along the slopes, including Cleonae, Thyssus, and Acrothoon, the last of which was renowned for the ripe old ages of its residents. Colonies consisting of Pelasgians set up camp on the foot of the mountain.

Alas, the citizens of the peninsula were far too materialistic and thankless for the Olympian gods' liking, so to teach the ingrates a lesson, the vindictive deities shook the peninsula with an apocalyptic earthquake that decimated every last city. Those who survived decamped to the mainland, and Athos remained largely vacant until 368 BCE, when it fell under the jurisdiction of the Macedonian King Philip II, later succeeded by his son, Alexander the Great. According to the works of Plutarch and Strabo, Dinocrates, the chief architect and the ambitious mastermind behind the city of Alexandria, began to conceive a design that would outshine Alexandria. The plan was to carve Mount Athos into the likeness of Alexander, leading some modern historians to refer to the idea as the "classical Greek Mount Rushmore." An entire city would be nestled upon the colossal sculpture's outstretched palm. Draped over his right shoulder and arm were streams and cascading waterfalls that would be linked to the Aegean Sea.

Such a magnificent monument would seem almost impossible to turn down, yet that is precisely what Alexander did. "Let the mountain stand as it is," was Alexander's alleged response to Dinocrates. "It is sufficient that another king perpetuated his arrogance by having a canal cut through it."

An ancient bust of King Philip II of Macedon

An 18th century imagination of what the monument would look like

Andrew Dunn's picture of an ancient bust of Alexander

This "arrogant" king was none other than Xerxes, the Persian emperor from the 5th century BCE best known for invading Greece during the Second Persian War. During the First Persian War, the Persians had a fleet badly damaged when it barreled into Athos' cragged coastline. Hoping to prevent a repeat of such a tragedy, Xerxes dispatched a crew of men to the peninsula and ordered them to create a canal that sliced through the isthmus between the mainland and Athos a decade later. This allowed later fleets to sail through the shortcut safely, as opposed to having to tackle the dicey southern point, Cape Akrothoos of the Athos peninsula. With the help of the canal, Xerxes successfully invaded the Greek mainland, but after the Battle of Salamis and the Battle of Plataea, the Persians were ultimately driven out of Greek terrain.

Whether this canal truly existed is still a matter of dispute, with some claiming the canal was only partially built before Xerxes's architects were made to abandon the project, and others asserting the project was never even started. Believers today point the cynical to the supposed dregs and remnants of the canal in its purported location on the peninsula, which hints at the one-time existence of an artificial channel.

D. Bachman's picture of the peninsula from the summit of Mount Athos

The Byzantine Era

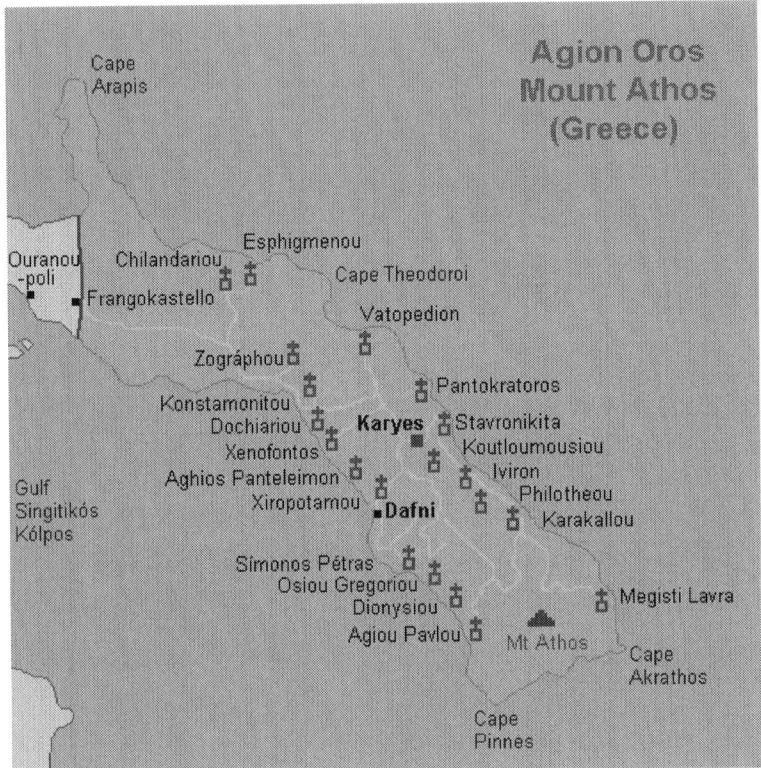

A map of various monasteries on the peninsula

"It is impossible to save one's soul without devotion to Mary and without her protection." – attributed to Anselm of Canterbury

Naturally, the Christian chapter of Mount Athos' history unfolded only after the beginning of the Common Era, and ironically, the ostensibly anti-woman culture within Athos, as maintained by its present locals, was conceived by a woman. According to the locals, that woman was none other than the mother of Jesus.

According to this account, in the summer of 49, Mary was invited to Cyprus by a post-resurrected Lazarus. To this, she readily agreed and boarded a small boat, but as fate would have it, a dreadful storm struck, steering the helpless vessel to the eastern coast of the Athonite peninsula, close to the present monastery of Iveron. The disoriented, but otherwise unhurt Mary staggered out of the broken boat. As soon as she took in the beauty of her surroundings, the soles of her feet sinking into the toasty sand, all panic and fear melted away. "This mountain is holy ground," she proclaimed to her son, her eyes fixed upon the mist cloaked over the Athonite peak. "Let it now be my portion. Here let me remain for eternity."

What happened next was nothing short of a miracle, one that could only be powered by the heavens. Once Mary started towards the slopes, the splendid temple devoted to Apollo, built on the Athonite summit, crumbled. This triggered a domino effect, and one by one, sculptures of pagan statues and other "false idols" either toppled over or disintegrated. Left standing amidst the rubble was the stone statue of Apollo on the peak of the mountain, which came to life and thundered across the peninsula: "Heed my words – I am a false idol. You must renounce me and come forth to pay tribute to the *Panaghia*, the true mother of God." With that, Apollo self-destructed.

Hermits and villagers alike did as they were ordered and came forth to honor their new matriarch. Each was baptized, cleansed of their pagan sins, and thenceforth tasked with carrying the Christian torch.

Author Gregory Palamas transcribed Mary's promissory speech to her new subjects in the *Life of St. Peter the Athonite*: "In Europe, there is a mountain, very high and very beautiful, which extends towards the south and very deeply into the sea. This is the mountain that I have chosen out of all the earth, and I have decided to make of it the country of the monastic order. I have consecrated it to be henceforth my dwelling: this is why people will call it the 'Holy Mountain.' All who shall come to live there after having decided to fight the battle against the common enemy of the human race will find me at their side throughout their lives…I will be their invincible aid, I will teach them what they must do, and what they must avoid. I myself shall be their tutor, their physician, their nurse. I shall take care to give them both food and the care that their bodies require, and that which is necessary for their souls, to inspire and invigorate them, so they depart not from virtue. And all who finish their lives on this mountain in a spirit of love for God and repentance, I promise to recommend to my Son and God that He accord them complete remission of their sins."

Despite Mary's alleged arrival in the 1st century CE, Orthodox Christianity did not enter the Athonite mainstream until the advent of the Byzantine Empire. It was only during the Council of Nicaea in 325 CE that this brand of Christianity was declared the official religion, and governmental headquarters were transferred to Byzantium, which would soon become Constantinople 5 years later. The Western Roman Empire collapsed in 476 CE, but its Eastern, predominantly Hellenistic counterpart in the Mediterranean – the Byzantine Empire – endured for almost another 1,000 years.

As determined by the Council of Chalcedon in 451 CE, the Christian world of the 5th century was split into five patriarchates, which were as follows: Rome, spearheaded by the pope as its patriarch; Antioch; Alexandria; Jerusalem; and Constantinople. Byzantine Emperor Flavius Marcian was appointed head of church and state for Constantinople, and Marcian's successors continued to reap the rewards of this title well into the 7th century, remaining the patriarch of the Eastern Orthodox Church even after the Muslim Saracens' capture of Antioch, Alexandria, and Jerusalem.

Riveting legends aside, knowledge of Athonite residents between prehistoric times and the 9th century CE is flimsy at best, if only because archaeologists are prohibited from digging or "desecrating" the hallowed land. Some historians believe that the first hermits in Athos were asylum seekers who fled during the Arab incursions into Byzantine territory, while others insist they were Iconodules (those who supported the controversial veneration of religious icons) shunned by Iconoclast emperors. Furthermore, there are the Virgin-deniers who insist that the natives were nonconforming recluses from nearby lands who were simply drawn to the unparalleled, and therefore magnetic solitude that Athos had to offer. Christian monks – some disgruntled by internal ecclesiastical corruptions and others simply looking for deeper spiritual fulfillment – eventually chanced upon the peninsula in the 4th century CE and took to the mountains to erect their new homes. At this stage, the Athonite monks lived hermetically, for the concept of communal monastic societies had only just been inaugurated in the Egyptian desert around this time. The tradition gradually spread across the Middle East before penetrating Europe sometime around the late 7th century or early 8th century.

By the year 843, according to the local 10th century historian Genesios, there was already a primitive, but well-established monastic community on Mount Athos. The community was composed mainly of a sizable group of monks who arrived in the early 700s and were present at the Seventh Ecumenical Council of Nicaea (also referred to as the Second Council of Nicaea) in 787. The conference revolved around the controversial issue of the era: icons and their place in Christian worship. This feud between the Iconodules and the Iconoclasts first arose in 726, when Emperor Leo III demanded the removal of Christ's portrait above Constantinople's Chalke Gate.

On the one hand, Iconoclasts were adamant that icon veneration defied Scripture, and some zealous Iconoclasts took such offense to the practice that they would sneak into private homes and churches to deface and dismantle these false idols in the name of God. As for the Iconodules, or Iconophiles, their counterargument is summed up by an excerpt provided by *Khan Academy*: "Images of Christ do not depict natures, being either divine or human, but a concrete person – Jesus Christ." They, did, however, concur when it came to outlawing depictions of God the Father: "God prohibited any representation of God (or anything that could be worshiped as a god) because it was impossible to depict the invisible God."

The discourse was heated, but in the end, the council ruled in favor of the Iconodules. The practice was to be restored, and artworks devoted to Christ and other saintly figures were proclaimed "open books to remind [one] of God." As stated by the verdict, "Icons...are to be kept in churches and honored with the same relative veneration as is shown to other material symbols, such as the 'precious and life-giving Cross' and the Book of the Gospels." 22 canons were simultaneously published. Canon 7 affirmed the necessary installation of relics in all churches, Canon 18 banned all women from lodging in monasteries and the houses of bishops, and Canon 20 forbade the establishment of "double" or co-ed monasteries.

Over time, the solitude the Athonite monks so prized was interrupted time and time again, both inadvertently and deliberately by external forces who yearned to claim the slice of paradise for themselves. The Battle of Thasos, fought in October of 829, concluded with the Cretan Arabs' triumph over the Byzantines. As reported by the *Theophanes Continuatus*, the official collection of annals commissioned by Emperor Constantine VII, the Byzantine navy was crushed, losing almost all of their warships. Thus, the Mediterranean, Mount Athos included, entered its first major dark age, and in the decades that followed, vulnerable Byzantine islands were subjected to a string of vicious raids carried out by Saracen generals and rogue pirates. With supplementary help from Byzantine Islam converts, the Saracens succeeded in seizing, destroying, and looting the Cyclades before directing their attention towards Mount Athos. The brutality of the ambushes that targeted the pitifully protected peninsula rendered it abandoned for a few decades.

This state of desertion ended in 860 with the arrival of Friar Efthymios the Younger, which coincided with the rise of Macedonian Emperor Basil I. The debris was cleared, the burned patches punctuating the land were replenished, and a small number of huts, known as the "Skiti of Saint Basil," were constructed around Efthymios' home by the *Krya Nera*, or the "Dark Spring," that trickled down from the mountain. With the blessings of the pious emperor, the retired Archbishop of Crete, Basil the Confessor, installed a modest monastery where the harbor of the Hilandar Monastery now stands.

The Hilandar Monastery in the 1890s

Much like the traumatized monks who were forced to vacate the peninsula during the Saracen raids, Emperor Basil was shattered by the mutilation of the Holy Mountain, and he was resolved to squash such a recurrence. In 883, Basil formally took the peninsula under his imperial wing when he issued a "gold-sealed" *sigillion* that banned all shepherds from grazing on the peninsula and inhibited all other potential intruders from entry. Not even state officials were allowed to set foot on Athos without permission. Two years later, Basil emancipated the Athonite monks from the dominion of the episcopal see in Hierissus, cementing the Athonites' authority over the *Agion Oros*.

The cenobitic lifestyle, which centered on communal living – namely, a society wherein everyone was assigned their own roles and expected to contribute equally – was most likely employed far earlier, but it only caught on amongst the Athonite monasteries in the mid-10th century. Interestingly, reception of this practice was initially split down the middle. There were those who championed the organization of monastic life, and formed monasteries in neighboring territories accordingly. On the opposite end of the spectrum were the anti-cenobites, who condemned the cenobites' rigid liturgical system, which fused the "solemn Liturgy of the Hours" with the practice of hourly prayer. They were instead proponents of more "moderate" nine-ode "structured canons," or "hymnography," which were segregated into different anthologies and chanted throughout scheduled liturgical cycles. Famous anti-cenobite St. Blasios of Amorion endeavored to usher in the more relaxed studite practice in the year 900, to no avail.

Following the death of Emperor Basil I in 908, the peninsula's residents found themselves paddling through gray waters yet again. The Athonites had to act swiftly, for rival monks from St. Colobos, near Hierissus, were once again flexing their jaws for the coveted Mount Athos. Fortunately, they managed to secure the protection of Basil's successor, Leo VI, and remained more or less an independent entity. 34 years later, Emperor Romanos I Lecapenos strengthened the imperial protection over Athos by extending an annual pension of one gold nugget each to the Athonite monks. Technically speaking, the monks were now "salaried public servants," so they were expected to pray for and bless the sovereign, his empire, and all their military campaigns.

By the 950s, the Athonites had already developed a functioning governing system, and even a set of legislation of their own. Seated within the uppermost level of the pyramid was the *Protos* (Premier), the governor of all Athonite monastic communities. The *protos* was charged with the representation of the peninsula in domestic and international affairs, and vested with a slew of managerial powers, such as the appointment and dismissal of abbots. Up until 1312, the *protos* was named by the emperor. All *protos* after the fact were elected by members of the *Iera Epistasia,* or "Holy Administration." This board of monastic executives, in turn, oversaw the *Iera Koinotita,* or "Holy Community," which comprised delegates from each of the peninsula's monasteries.

More titles were added to the *Protaton* in Karyes, the administrative capital of Athos, between the latter half of the 10th and the early 11th centuries. Such posts include the *oikonomos* (household-manager), the *ecclesiarchis* (sacristans), and the *epitiritis* (procurator). The governing body convened in Karyes on three occasions each year – Christmas, Easter, and the Feast of the Koimesis of the Virgin on August 15th) – in conferences called *"synaxes"* to dissect the most pressing and contentious issues.

The arrival of Saint Athanasios the Athonite in 957 marked the dawn of another new age on the peninsula. Accompanying Athanasios, a former teacher from Constantinople, was future Emperor Nikephoros II, at the time a general. Together, the fierce duo succeeded in staving off multiple Saracen invasions. Five years later, Athanasios directed the refurbishment of the main church in Karyes. Following Nikephoros' ascension to the imperial throne in 963, secured through his politically motivated betrothal to Empress Theophano, he conquered Candia and regained Crete later that year. Profits from his conquest of Candia were used to fund what was known as the "Great Lavra" in the fall of 963. The Great Lavra was the concentration of the existing "scattered" monasteries into one monastic community, an institution that would reign superior within the Athonite community. During the imperial reign of Nikephoros, the lavra began to deviate from its humble beginnings. As Nicholaos Economidis of *Elpenor* put it, the lavra "was transformed into a lavishly endowed royal foundation for approximately 80 monks, with annual revenues in cash and kind and with lands and property exempt from taxation."

An icon of St. Athanasios

The Great Lavra, the grandest *koinobion* ("common life") monastery constructed by the Byzantine Empire thus far, boasted such innovative designs and methodical structure that its model was replicated by numerous monasteries within and outside of Mount Athos. Bearing this in mind, the Great Lavra was pioneering in more ways than one, for it was the first monastery to be granted independence from the Patriarch of Constantinople, along with the right to name its own bishop. These important new liberties were outlined in the three chrysobulls issued by

Nikephoros in 964. On top of their newfound independence, the lavra was formally guaranteed a pension of 244 gold pieces each year, as well as a substantial consignment of wheat.

A medieval depiction of Nikephoros

Athanasios personally superintended the compound's construction, which, upon its unveiling, featured the Basilica of the Theotokos, as well as individual cells, fountains, a refectory, hostel, kitchen, and a number of other amenities. The population of the complex only continued to rise over the years, escalating to 120 in less than a decade; halfway into the 11th century, that number soared to 700.

Seated close to the southeastern tongue of the peninsula, the Great Lavra, otherwise known as the "Monastery of Megisti Lavra," remains the oldest and grandest of all the Athonite monasteries. For a complex nearly 1,500 years old, the lavra remains in near pristine condition, save for the natural wear and tear prompted by the salty air. To the untrained eye, the enclosure seems more like a tiny, compact town, with a 15-tower fortress that guarded the complex and the treasures inside its 37 chapels and massive library, which housed over 30,000 printed books, 2,046 manuscripts, and 165 original codices. Also included in the lavra's spectacular relic collection were the *sakkos* and crown of Emperor Nikephoros, as well as the body of Athonasias himself, buried in the Chapel of Forty Martyrs.

Mates II's picture of the Great Lavra

The *katholikon* of the monastery

The *katholikon*, or central church of the Great Lavra also served as the archetype of all future *katholika* erected on Mount Athos. Consecrated to the Annunciation of the Blessed Virgin Mary, the four-columned, cross-shaped structure consisted of only two stories, and was topped by a ribbed, hemispherical dome garnished with wavy edges. The first Athonite *Phiale*, a studded libation bowl constantly filled with holy water, was installed by the main entrance of the *katholikon*. In the 1400s, the Grand Lavra was reconsecrated, this time dedicated to a post-canonized Athanasios. The Lavra underwent routine renovations the following century, with the most significant addition being the colorful frescoes of biblical scenes and detailed portrait medallions of saints painted onto the walkway and the arched roof of the refectory in 1535. This was the work of Cretan painter and monk Theophanes Strelitsa, whose glowing portfolio included artwork found in the Meteora monasteries. The decision to coat the entire facade with red paint was made at a later date.

A fresco at Mount Athos depicting Saint Mercurius and Artemius of Antioch

Athanasios's pride in perfecting the Athonite way of life is reflected in the *Typikon*, a book listing the rubric for the religious services in 973, the year he authored it. "I have found by experience that it is right and beneficial...for all the brothers to live in common. All together they are to look to the same goal of salvation...They form one heart in their common life, one will, one desire, and one body, as the apostle prescribes."

As previously mentioned, the majority of the hermits openly resisted the intervention, as mankind tends to be when confronted with change. The studites resented the severity of the new worshiping customs, which included forced punctuality and maintaining absolute silence throughout these droning divine services. Others criticized the uncharacteristic extravagance of the compound, complete with bustling workshops, for it contradicted the very essence of the material-free solitude attached to conventional hermeticism.

Evidently, all protests were made in vain, for Nikephoros's successor, Emperor John I Tzimiskes, ultimately put the ball in the cenobites' court. In 972, the Great Lavra was issued its first official charter, called the *"Tragos,"* which legitimized a regime that centered on the "coexistence of both traditional eremitic monasticism and the new cenobite system." The same charter also created the post of the *hegumens*, "spiritual fathers" or chief confessors of the different monastic communities, and rolled out a new set of rules all Athonite monks were to abide by.

Economidis explored some of these said rules in the following passage: "Solitary reclusion [sic] was permitted only to experienced monks, who were in addition required to observe a certain discipline...peregrination was not permitted. The *Tragos* further defined...the economic and social relations between hermits and monks, and monks and lay folk. Compulsory unpaid labor was abolished, and discipline was imposed on relations between monks: any who were quarrelsome were liable to be expelled." Furthermore, "the numbers of cattle owned by the foundations was severely restricted: only the Great Lavra...was permitted to own a yoke of oxen (for the purpose of kneading...bread)."

By the time the 10th century drew to a close, the bulk of the most prominent Athonite monasteries – including the Hilander, Vatopedi, Iveron, and Panteleimon, amongst others – had been established. There were a total of 46 monasteries on the peninsula (one source claims there was as many as 3,000).

The 10th century was also underscored by the active adoption of a law that would lead to what is arguably the most salient and delicate of the peninsula's present controversies. Included in the 10th century *Tragos* was a canon that called for the expulsion of all female animals on Mount Athos. Female cows, goats, dogs, ewes, and every other native mammal were banished from Athonite grounds, so as to never "defile [the eyes of the monks] with anything female." Only insects, birds, and cats (favored for their rodent-ridding abilities) were exempt from this rule. Needless to say, while it wasn't specified in this particular charter, it was second nature for women to avoid the peninsula. It wasn't until 1046 that Canon 18, issued by the Second Council of Nicaea in 787, was reiterated in the chrysobull of Emperor Constantine Monomachos. Monomachos' bull also ordered all eunuchs and young boys to avoid Athos, for their "effeminate character" could serve as a source of temptation for the celibate monks.

Though the absence of carnal temptations is most likely the main motivator behind the peninsula's prohibition of women, most Athonite monks will claim otherwise. They are merely observers of an uncompromising rule laid down by the Blessed Mother herself. Dr. Graham Speake, author of *Mount Athos: Renewal in Paradis*, explained, "It's still called 'the garden of the mother of God,' dedicated to her glory, and she alone represents her sex on [the peninsula]." This rule was made even more cogent by the alleged succession of divine Marian apparitions that (conveniently) materialized before the Athonite monks in the years following the publication of the 1046 chrysobull. To this day, the only women allowed on the peninsula are the Virgin Mary and select female saints, captured in the frescoes of the Athonite monasteries.

Endless Battles

"The soul that has come to know God fully no longer desires anything else, nor does it attach itself to anything on this earth; and if you put before it a kingdom, it would not desire it, for the love of God gives such sweetness and joy to the soul that even the life of a king can no longer give it any sweetness." – Silouan the Athonite

The magnanimity the Byzantine rulers exhibited towards the Athonite monks has since been attributed to a number of political motivations. An unspoken rapport was forged between the royals and the monks, with the latter beholden to the emperors on account of their generous donations. The emperors further enhanced the relationship between them by gifting Athonite authorities sweeping territories in the Halkidiki outside of Athos, as well as in Thessaloniki, which became dependencies of the Athonite establishments.

Profits and goods produced by the monks' multiple dependencies ensured that their basic needs were fulfilled. For example, Athonites from the 12th century were reportedly so invested in the thriving wine trade in the Halkidiki, which was eventually woven into the peninsula's culture, that it incited great outcry from hordes of monks. Among the most vocal detractors of the monasteries' wine obsession was Efstathios, who served as the Archbishop of Thessaloniki between 1180 and 1195. He lamented, "[The Athonite monks] deliberate more on the vine than on theology."

Following the sack of Constantinople in 1204 during the Fourth Crusade in 1204, Mount Athos fell into the hands of the short-lived Frankish Kingdom of Thessaloniki ("Thessalonica"). This abrupt transition resulted in the loss of several Athonite properties outside of the peninsula, and though the kingdom was dissolved just 20 years later, they would not regain ownership of the properties in question until 1261, when the power of Constantinople was restored.

Once Mount Athos was again subjugated to the Byzantine Empire, local monks implored for peace, but regrettably, their prayers went unanswered. The obstinate Emperor Michael VIII Palaiologos was disliked by the Athonites from the very beginning, but it was his orchestration of the 1274 Union of Lyons, otherwise known as the "Second Council of Lyons," that most provoked the indignant wrath of the Athonite monks. His open persecution of the Athonite monks who objected to the council's verdict – which called for the end of the Great Schism that separated the Eastern Orthodox Church from the Roman Catholic Church – only aggravated the aggrieved monks.

Tensions between Emperor Michael VIII Palaiologos and the Athonites continued to decay, reaching a crescendo four years later when the emperor promulgated a decree that called for the marriage of these Churches at Constantinople, regardless of the permission of both parties. The reputation of John XI Bekkos, then the Ecumenical Patriarch of Constantinople, was no better; the holy man was branded a traitor by the Athonites when he voiced his support for the union.

A 14th century depiction of Emperor Michael VIII Palaiologos

After wrapping up their campaigns in the Holy Land, the Crusaders returned to Byzantine lands and pledged their services to Emperor Michael VIII Palaiologos. Turkish and Tartar soldiers-for-hire were also prepared to enforce Michael's proclamation, should the situation call for it.

The Athonites, as one might expect, were outraged by the authoritarian proclamation, and duly expressed their discontent in a withering letter. They wrote, "We clearly see that you [Emperor Michael] are becoming a heretic, but we implore you to forsake all this and abide in the teachings that were handed down to you...Reject the unholy and novel teachings of a false knowledge [in reference to the Latin Church], speculations, and additions to the Faith." They vehemently made clear their perpetual opposition against numerous doctrines upheld by the Catholic Church, such as the supremacy of and devotion displayed towards the pope, their distortion of the Holy Creed, and their utilization of "unleavened bread" as the Body of Christ, amongst other offenses.

The emperor bared his teeth, but the resolve of the Athonite monks did not waver, which only seemed to further incense the emperor. Indisposed to antagonizing his new Greek subjects, the prejudiced emperor – as portrayed by Orthodox sources – relieved his frustrations by tormenting the Bulgarian monks in the Zograf Monastery on the southwestern part of Mount Athos. In the autumn of 1284, a vicious contingent of armed Crusaders stormed into Zograf, presenting them with a chilling ultimatum: accept the Union of Lyons, or face the fatal consequences.

The Zograf Monastery

The spirits of the Zograf monks remained unbroken, but the better part of the brotherhood eventually filed out of the complex to avoid further hostilities. 26 held out in the monastery's tallest tower, and when the Catholic soldiers ordered them to vacate the premises once again, they refused to budge, seemingly resigned to their inevitable fates. On the 10th of October, the soldiers set the tower ablaze, and all 26 – including Friars Igumen Thomas, Cyril, Barsanuphius, Sava, Martinian, Cyprian, Parthenius, Joasaph, along with four other unnamed laymen – perished in the flames, giving their lives for the Orthodox cause.

The tempestuous relationship between the Catholics and Greek Orthodox remained as such until the latter part of the 14th century. Much of the relief is attributed to the Kydones brothers – elder brother, Demetrios, a wildly popular statesman who served three terms as *Mesazon* (Imperial Premier) for the Byzantine Empire, and younger brother, Prochoros, an Athonite monk and theologian. Together, the talented linguists converted a series of religious Latin texts into Greek, such as the *Mesazon's* translation of Saint Thomas's *Summa contra Gentiles*. This passage from the *Dialogos Institute* illustrates what ensued: "[Demetrios] helped to bring about the reconciliation of...Emperor John V Palaiologos with the Holy See. In 1369, the Emperor and *Mesazon* traveled to Rome in person and professed the common faith of [the] east and west in Saint Peter's Basilica. Prochoros, a monk of Mount Athos, would later suffer persecution for his witness to the simplicity of the Godhead..."

The disagreements that developed within the monastic community on Mount Athos included the issue of being consecrated to a scholarly life on the peninsula. Initially, the majority of Athonite monks during this period found the growing treasury of texts impractical and pointless, if only because they were chiefly illiterate and educated only in the arts of austerity and spirituality gained through stringent self-discipline. It was only around the mid-14th century that this consensus faded. Athonite monks, encouraged by the influx of new, well-read monks, lowered their guards and began to dust off the precious literature in their monasteries. Not only did they begin to procure even more sacred manuscripts, a few monasteries – such as the Hilander and the Iveron – established *scriptoria* of their own and churned out their own texts. Soon, a cross-cultural network of intellectuals and creative spirits was developed within the peninsula, one colored by theologians, musical composers, hagiographers (biographers of saints), and ecclesiastical chroniclers. In addition to the Iveron and the Hilandar, the Panteleemon and Zograf Monasteries became vibrant academic hubs that functioned as distribution centers of religious texts to Bulgaria, Serbia, Georgia, and Russia.

The Iveron Monastery

It was during this time that the future Saint Gregory of Sinai, a displaced monk who made his home in Athos in 1310, divulged to the Athonites the mystical "Jesus prayer," a short incantation he learned from a Friar Arsenios in Crete: "Lord Jesus Christ, have mercy on me, a sinner." The charismatic Gregory managed to reel in a small, but ultimately high-yielding quantity of monks with the unconventional ideas of mysticism he peppered into his daily devotions, and he is therefore credited with introducing Hesychasm to the peninsula. Archbishop of Thessaloniki, esteemed theologian, and former Athonite monk Gregory Palamas heartily backed the esoteric teachings of Gregory of Sinai, and the trend of Hesychasm quickly gained traction, so much so that it was formally incorporated into the Orthodox doctrine in 1351.

Unfortunately, the blossoming prosperity of Mount Athos was bittersweet, because once their collections of literary gems and sacred relics continued to swell, unwanted attention from gluttonous outlanders increased accordingly. Callous convoys of marauding pirates from Asia Minor were among the first to descend upon Mount Athos between the late 12th century and early 13th century. The savage, sword-wielding pirates were so relentless that large bodies of Athonite monks began to teem out of the peninsula, seeking solace and refuge in the nearby cities of Meteora and Paroria instead. Moreover, the Byzantine Civil War, which dragged on between 1341 and 1347, saw the destruction of Thrace and Macedonia, along with the heinous slaughter of hundreds or perhaps even thousands of residents. Numerous Athonite monasteries suffered another spell of pillaging during this turbulent time.

In 1345, in the midst of the civil war, Serbian king Stefan Dušan captured the Macedonian city of Sérres and declared himself Emperor of the Serbs and Greeks. Stefan Uroš V, the heir to the imperial crown, went on to claim ownership of the peninsula, allotting different portions of the land to various divisions within the Serbian Empire. The crippled Byzantine authorities were disconcerted, to say the least, by the bold changes being made by the Serbians, but despite their best efforts, they were unable to reverse these actions. As such, the Serbian Empire continued to reign over Mount Athos until 1371.

To the disappointment of the Byzantine imperials, their control over Eastern Macedonia would soon collapse. Emperor John and his retinue scrambled to plug the holes rapidly sprouting along the sides of the sinking ship, which included an attempt to marshal an army with relics seized from the Athonite monasteries, but they failed to fend off the new, more menacing opponent on the horizon. In 1383, Ottoman Turkish forces conquered Sérres and seized Mount Athos soon thereafter.

As steadfastly faithful as the Athonites were to their principles, they knew it was time to recalibrate their defensive strategies. Fearing the loss of their monastic society altogether, the insightful monks went into survival mode. They had no delusions about their lackluster security – a sobering reality crystallized by their lack of defenses against the pirate attacks – and understood that their survival hinged on the protection and patronage of whoever bore the imperial crown. As narrated by a 16th century historian named "Muned/d/imbas/zi," a band of Orthodox representatives from the Pridromos Monastery near Sérres was assembled and sent to appeal to Sultan Orkhan (or Orhan) for an "*affirman*," or a guarantee of protection. The Athonite monks followed in their Macedonian brothers' footsteps years later, acquiring the guardianship and other privileges from Orkhan's successor, Sultan Murad I. Philotheos Kokkinos, who served as Ecumenical Patriarch of Constantinople for nearly three consecutive terms in the mid-14th century, confirmed the Ottomans' "support...and admiration," as well as the charity they exhibited towards the Athonite monks in his 1360 homily. This fruitful tactic, which entailed remaining in the good graces of those who posed the greatest threat, would not be lost on the future generations of Athonites.

Even with the Ottomans in their corner, Athonite monasteries saw a rather drastic decline in their population in the years leading up to the 1400s. This decline, many believe, led to the monasteries' gradual retirement of the cenobitic lifestyle. Instead, many Athonite institutions began to embrace the so-called "idiorrhythmic," or "self-regulating" system. Plainly put, while Athonite monks continued to belong to brotherhoods, they no longer lived collectively, but in privately-owned, often remotely situated cells. In addition to their new ability to obtain and maintain personal assets, a nostalgic sense of independence and true solitude was reinstated. Athonites who adhered to the idiorrhythmic system were expected to rear their own crops, secure their own supplies, repair their own clothes and furniture, and so forth. They spent the bulk of their days confined to their cells, only breaking away from their lodgings to attend services at a nearby *katholikon*. While the new monastic arrangement alienated many of the peninsula's residents, it also lured in a considerable number of aspiring monks from aristocratic backgrounds who were previously repelled by the rigidness of cenobitic monasticism.

By 1430, it was clear that the Ottomans were not going away anytime soon. In a surprising turn of events, however, the *Agion Oros* – which was, up to this point, seemingly under the permanent jurisdiction of the Turkish Sultan – was granted autonomy. In return, Athonite authorities agreed to surrender their territories in Macedonia and Thrace, as well as a few other privileges, and cough up a yearly tax for the continued protection of the Ottomans.

In the wake of the Ottomans' conquest of Constantinople and the dissolution of the Byzantine Empire, the Athonites continued to prosper under Turkish rule. Ottoman sultans and other affluent members of Turkish society began to entrust their valuables – mostly artwork, but some say, a few chests bursting with gold, silver, and jewels – to the Athonite monks, who carefully stowed them away in their monasteries for safekeeping. Apart from the compensation they received for the storage of said valuables, the most distinguished monasteries continued to be presented with regular donations. Monasteries dipped into their funds, further strengthening their fortifications.

The new commercial twists applied to Athonite customs solidified the new idiorrhythmic character that had developed within this small, free-form strip of land. Not only were monasteries accepting gratuities in exchange for prayers, blessings, and art-storage – even from those who had no intentions of visiting the monastery – Athonite institutions revived the viticultural trade and dabbled in other enterprises. For a parcel of land or a sum of 100 gold pieces, for instance, the monks pledged to provide their benefactors with predetermined quantities of wine, oil, cheese, legumes, wheat, tomatoes, peppers, and a host of other herbs and produce until the donor's death, delivered periodically and in batches. Though some complained about the impiety of making a profit, most made their peace with the practice, for they were, in their eyes, simply maximizing on surplus crops that would have otherwise gone to waste.

Furthermore, the increase in territorial and monetary donations resulted in the construction, as well as the structural and cosmetic rehabilitation of more monasteries on the peninsula. Among the reconditioned monasteries was Konstamonitou, a small, 10th-century compound funded in part by both Byzantine emperors and Serbian princes. The Konstamonitou was famous for its brick-red roof, its library of 100 rare codices, and for providing shelter to the icons of Saint Stephen and the *Panagia Hodgetria Antiphonetria.* Another was the Koutloumousiou. Originally founded in 1169, the square complex was renovated in the time of Abbot Chariton of Imbros, financed by a pair of Wallachian princes and other nobles along the Danube River. The *katholikon* of Koutloumousiou, dedicated to the Transfiguration of Christ, was constructed during the makeover, but was only embellished with frescoes in 1744. Today, the Koutloumousiou places sixth in the pyramid of Athonite monasteries.

The Konstamonitou

There were also some new monasteries raised, including the Monastery of Gregoriou, also known as the "Osiou Grigoriou Monastery." This triple-tiered, stern-looking stone structure was built upon a rocky protrusion right by the edge of the southwestern coast. It was designed in 1310 by Gregory the Young, the hesychast disciple of Saint Gregory of Sinai, and dedicated to Nicholas of Myra, the patron saint of sailors and merchants.

Rudolf Bauer's picture of the Osiou Grigoriou Monastery

The Monastery of Pantokratoros, between the Monasteries of Vatopedi and Iveron, was erected on the fringe of the peninsula's eastern coast in 1357. The complex, shaped like a slightly skewed trapezoid, was founded by two brothers known only as Alexios, *Megas Stratopedarches* (Grand Master of the Camp) for the Byzantine military, and John, the *Megas Primikerios* (Chief Lector of a Monastery). The Pantokrator, which originally harbored the Christ icon now displayed in St. Petersburg, boasted a handsome *katholikon* and 15 chapels. It quickly rose to prominence within the Athonite hierarchy, placing 15th by 1394.

The Pantokratoros

By the end of the 14th century, every monastery on the peninsula was sponsored by at least one wealthy noble. It became a tacit, but common practice for imperial and federal leaders to financially buttress one Athonite monastery apiece. These patrons saw it as a personal call of duty of sorts, for only then, they believed, could they ensure that their souls, along with those of their subjects, would be saved.

In 1424, the Athonites relied again on their diplomatic skills to shield themselves from the usual hassles and potential complications that typically came with a change in regime. That spring, a company of Athonite monks traveled to Adrianopolis ("Edirne") in East Thrace and successfully brokered another arrangement of patronage with Sultan Murad II. Ironically, the Athonites had sought the assent of Byzantine Emperor Manuel II Palaiologos prior to scheduling the meeting, but while the Athonites are most renowned for their homely, rustic lives, they were keenly aware of the stormy political climate and understood that they could not afford to lose any of their patrons, whether the patrons were Byzantine emperors, Ottoman nobles, or Danubian princes. Put simply, they strove to pave new paths, but they also made sure not to burn existing bridges.

There is plenty of evidence that showcases the continued camaraderie between the Athonites and Constantinople, even under Turkish rule. The Synod of Florence, otherwise known as the "Council of Florence," convened in that Italian city in between 1438 and 1439. A few weeks before the ecumenical conference, which was the Catholic Church's second attempt to merge with the Greek Orthodox, Emperor John VIII Palaiologos sent a team of delegates to Mount Athos for duplicates of reference codices and religious law books no longer available in Constantinople. The emperor also consulted with Athonite elders, and he was so dependent on their wisdom that he invited an assemblage of monks to the council to represent the Byzantine side.

The growing popularity of Hesychasm on Mount Athos, however, split the Orthodox Christians of 14th century Byzantine society. One camp praised the mystic system, and the other stigmatized the practice as bizarre and sinfully occult. The fundamentals of this system are briefly described in the following passage from Mitchell B. Liester's *Hesychasm: A Christian Path of Transcendence*: "[Hesychasts (practitioners of Hescyhasm)] encouraged individual experiences of the divine...[Hesychasts] describe two types of consciousness: ego-centered and ego-transcendent. The former is a state dominated by attachments to the senses, emotions, intellect, and imagination. The latter involves detachment from those faculties...The ultimate goal for Hesychasts is union with God."

Liester expands on the three steps required to reach this goal: "The first is dispassion (*apatheia*), which involves detachment from the senses and the emotions. The second is stillness (*hesychia*), which requires detachment from the discursive intellect and the imagination. The final step is an abiding state of illumination called 'deification' or 'perfect union with God' (*theosis*)."

Advocates, mainly from the Greek portion of the Eastern Church, defended the system, citing its alignment with the gospel revealed by the "apparitions of divine light" during the Transfiguration on Mount Tambor. Dialogue surrounding the delicate subject was conducted on three separate Synods – the Councils of 1341, 1347, and 1351 - but since the system had the backing of the Byzantine emperors themselves, Hesychasm triumphed on all three occasions. In the years that followed, a wave of Hesychast practitioners, including Gregory Palamas, Makarios Makris, Germanos the Athonite, among others, were proclaimed saints by the Orthodox Church.

Fascinating Friars

"When there is a respect for small things, there will be an even greater respect towards the bigger things." – attributed to Saint Paisios of Athos

To the monks on Mount Athos, prayer is life. Prayers and incantations were quite literally injected into every waking minute of their day. For starters, Athonite monks attended tediously rambling services that lasted anywhere between 5-8 hours a day, all 365 days of the year. Services were customarily prolonged on special feast days and religious celebrations; on Christmas, for example, the Athonite monks cooped themselves up in their churches for at least 15 consecutive hours.

The interior of the Athonite *katholikon*, the heart and soul of these monasteries, is breathless, consisting of ornate, gilded candelabras, majestic frescoes, priceless portraits, and intricate gold-leaf embellishments. The aromatic fragrance of frankincense and a medley of other nuances, emanating from the *livani* (Orthodox incense sticks) only elevates the sense of serenity. It was inside of these striking churches that the Athonite monks spent the better part of their days.

Most of the Athonite monasteries scheduled their services in the evening, sometimes as late as 2:00 a.m., because the more deafening the silence, the more effective their prayer. Towards the end of service, it was tradition for one of the higher-ranking monks to present to the congregation a number of the monastery's most prized relics, encased in separate silver reliquaries. Members of the brotherhood, as well as present pilgrims, formed a queue, with each granted an opportunity to plant a kiss on these miracle-inducing relics.

To this day, no modern instruments or backing tracks are used in Athonite services. Not only do modern monks find the usage of such accompaniments distracting, they strive to parallel their lives with those of the saints and martyrs of past centuries. As a result, most Athonites use only their voices to create music, which have made them master harmonizers, and instruments from the Byzantine era are used periodically. Moreover, only hymns from centuries-old songbooks are chorused.

The unceasing praying also continues outside of their respective *katholikon*, as the lips of an Athonite are perpetually dancing with monotonous, under-the-breath chants. Most recite either the "Jesus Prayer" or "*Kyrie eleison*" ("Lord, have mercy"). The habit is so deeply embedded among even the modern Athonite monks that they are able to wordlessly mouth these chants as they perform their daily duties.

Incessant praying aside, Athonite monks throughout history kept themselves preoccupied with the daily tasks and roles assigned to them, usually by the abbots. Cenobitic and idiorrhythmic monks alike were typically given positions that corresponded with their fortes, as well as a series of jobs, known collectively as *diakonimata* (obedience/offerings), that they were expected to complete weekly. Those with a knack for the culinary arts were appointed cooks, while wordsmiths were appointed scribes, hagiographers, and historical chroniclers. Those gifted with green thumbs were made managers of gardens and vineyards. The medically trained became doctors and worked out of small clinics in the monasteries. Daily tasks included beekeeping, fishing, and carpentry, as well as cleaning and maintenance work. They were, in sum, self-sufficient.

A separate department was created for the preservation and cataloging of the artwork and relics the monasteries had amassed. All in all, the Athonite monasteries are estimated to have procured a staggering 20,000 icons and 15,000 manuscripts, as well as dozens upon dozens of cabinets overflowing with costly crucifixes, bejeweled chalices, exquisite embroidery, and other irreplaceable fortunes.

The monks' distinctive dietary habits also separated the Athonites from the rest of the Greek Orthodox monks. To begin with, the Athonite brothers of the Byzantine Era were among the first to practice what can partially be described as "intermittent fasting," about 200 days each year. On Tuesdays, Thursdays, Saturdays, and Sundays, classified as "non-fasting days," the monks ate twice a day (once at about 11:00 a.m., and again at around 7:00 p.m.). On "abstention," or "fasting days," they ate only once, usually at dusk. On these days, their simple meals were restricted to plates of vegetables, fruit, lentils, or plain bread, and wine, milk, cheese, and the use of olive oil were to be avoided. All Athonite monks were either strict vegetarians or pescatarians.

Three "knocks" on the *semantron* – usually an unadorned percussion instrument reminiscent of a paddle, found in the arcade – summoned the Athonite monks to the refectory. They ate for only 10 minutes at a time, wolfing down their meals and downing the wines in their goblets in complete silence. There was no chit-chat allowed, because they were instead supposed to listen intently to the prayers or hagiographies recited by an elder monk. Only on non-abstention days were the monks allowed fish fried in olive oil, complete with a side of vegetables consisting of garden-fresh herbs.

The season of Great Lent is regarded as the most significant fasting period in the Orthodox Church, and Angelos Rentoulas noted the importance of this season in his 2016 article, "Fasting and Feasting on Mount Athos." "This is a period of preparation for Christians, both spiritual and physical, an exercise in spiritual upliftment which helps purify them so they can celebrate the feast of the Resurrection." Athonite chefs made certain to tweak their cooking methods in accordance with the rules of Athonite abstention during these 40 days. For example, they replaced olive oil with *tahini* (sesame paste), and only certain shellfish and mollusks were consumed on Great Lent.

Perhaps unsurprisingly, more often than not, Athonite monks had extremely clean bills of health and frequently outlived the laymen in the mainland. Researchers who were intrigued by the monks' disciplined diets conducted a study on the physical conditions of the Athonite monks. A total of 1,500 monks participated in the study between the years of 1994 and 2007. Of the 1,500 monks, not a single one tested positive for bowel or lung cancer, and only 11, representing 0.73% of the subjects, were diagnosed with prostate cancer. Haris Aidonopoulos, a urologist at the University of Thessaloniki, explained, "What seems to be the key is a diet that alternates between olive oil and non-olive oil days, and plenty of plant proteins. It's not only what we call the 'Mediterranean diet,' but also eating the old-fashioned way. Simple meals at regular intervals are very important."

The millennium-old diet is only one reason the Athonites live longer. After all, monks on the peninsula are afforded plenty of exercise thanks to the manual labor of harvesting ripe crops, kneading bread, transporting hefty building materials, and other daily tasks. Furthermore, the voluntary seclusion of the Athonite monks has shielded them from the stress that came with the ills of the outside world.

Modern monks are equally, if not more sheltered than their predecessors. Save for a few phones, a couple of cars, and other basic technology deemed mandatory in the 21st century, the Internet-deprived monks remained consciously ignorant of the current events and political crises that transpired beyond the borders. Libraries also remained free of newspapers, magazines, and any other non-religious or technical literature. In an interview with *60 Minutes*, an Athonite elder from the Simonopetra Monastery claimed that the brothers remained unaware of most, if not all important events, such as 9/11, until several years after the fact. Some today are supposedly still oblivious.

Sketes began to develop in full as the Athonites eased into the idiorrhythmic system, and monks who preferred a more hermetical lifestyle could opt for residence at one of these skete communities. These were not so much complexes as they were cells or "huts" loosely placed around a small central church known as the *"kyriakon."* Such an arrangement was ideal for more introverted souls who desired to be allotted their alone time, yet all the while still maintaining some form of social life through communal worship at the *kyriakon*. As each skete was affiliated to a cenobitic monastery, idiorrhythmic monks relied on the crops or farmland provided to them by the institution for food.

There are a dozen sketes on the peninsula today, the oldest being St. Anne, an affiliate of the Great Lavra. Much like the sketes of the olden days, present communities are overseen by a prior, or a "Fair," an official elected yearly by the elders of the skete.

The New Skete of the Agiou Pavlou monastery

Those who yearned for absolute solitude were directed to the monastic cells sprinkled across the slopes of the Holy Mountain. Cells were individual, often shoddily-built shacks inserted into the nooks and crannies on the face of a cliff. As of 1661, these cell clusters, or hermitages, were obliged by law to associate themselves with a monastery. Similar to skete communities, the affairs of these extreme hermetic compounds were governed by an elder and his spiritual cortége.

The Karoulia Hermitage is by far the most isolated and treacherously situated of all the Athonite hermitages. This is where 10 dauntless hermits reside in single-room huts and claustrophobic caves dangling over the discordant waves on the southwestern cliff face of Mount Athos, described as the "harshest part" of the range.

The first Karoulia hermits certainly took asceticism to an entirely new level. Rarely did these hermits leave their humble abodes, if only because their lone mode of transportation was a rickety pulley system consisting of man-sized baskets and a network of chains and ropes that allowed the monks to haul themselves from one point to the other. Those who were unable to "commute" on their own had to raise a bright flag, thus literally flagging down their neighbors for assistance. The pulley system, as implied by the name of the hermitage – *karoulia* being the Greek word for pulleys – was first perfected by the community on this cliff face.

For food, hermits lowered their baskets to levels populated by cenobitic monks and pilgrims. The baskets were then filled with a loaf of bread, some cheese, or olives. Jugs were used to collect rainwater dripping from nearby cavities.

The burial practice of the Athonite monks is yet another enthralling facet of the culture that developed within the peninsula. To start with, each Athonite monastery was equipped with a charnel house, or a plain vault erected closed to or underneath the *katholikon*. Upon the death of a brother, his corpse was swathed in a *schema* (the ceremonial robes sported by *"schemamonks"*), and his head covered with a *koukoulion*, an elaborate headdress featuring a pill-shaped crown with eared veils that draped over their shoulders. The corpse was then inserted into a cassock – the full-length robes worn by common Athonite monks – which was then sewn shut, acting as a kind of cloth coffin. Last, but not least, a blessed portrait of the Virgin Mary was placed atop the chest of the corpse.

After the funerary service, the cocooned body was transferred to a grave on a small square of cemetery land next to the monastery. Next, the grave was filled and a wooden, "four-pointed cross" was planted onto the freshly-packed earth. The name and date of death of the deceased was then painted onto the cross.

As dictated by tradition, Athonite brotherhoods prayed passionately and without rest for the deceased for a period of no less than 40 days. Day in and day out, the monks fingered the 33 knots on the cables of prayer ropes entangled around their palms, dutifully reciting the appropriate prayers. Monastery cooks also whipped up a platter of *kolivo*, a "memorial dish...[made from] wheat, rye, oat, or rice, as well as honey, raisins, and nuts."

The intensity of the memorial prayers wound down after those 40 days, but for the next three years, the monastery continued to make mention of the deceased at every Liturgy. The memory of the deceased was also immortalized in a safely-kept memorial book known as the "*Kuvaras*," which contained the names of all the brothers who died since the founding of the institution.

Three years after the monk's passing, his corpse was exhumed from the recycled grave, and experts then stepped forward to inspect the remains. Those with chunks of flesh still clinging to the bones were reburied, while only those that had withered away into bones were collected and prepped for the next stage. Failure to decompose in a timely manner is regarded by superstitious Athonites as proof of the dead's impurity, or lack of discipline in monastic life during his time on Earth. As such, their concerned brothers rolled up their sleeves and reinforced their prayers for him.

Bones of satisfactorily decomposed monks were first rinsed off in concoctions mainly of water and wine before they were transferred to the charnel house. The skulls were, likewise, dried off and transferred to the monastery's ossuary. As this excerpt from *The Catalog of Good Deeds* noted, "[T]he peculiarity of this crypt [lay] in the fact that the deceased, or rather, their remains, are not hidden there, but are in plain sight: the skulls are lined up in rows along the shelves, while the other bones are neatly laid right on the floor along the walls." Some skulls are stacked on top of one another in heaps.

Athonite monasteries also engaged in the tradition of skull-painting. Most complexes, such as the Skete Prophet Elias, opted for the power of simplicity and painted only names and years of birth and death on the foreheads of these skulls. The more artistic Athonites – such as those in the Russian Monastery of Saint Panteleimon, hailed as the "Rembrandts of skull-painting" – used the skulls as canvases for brilliantly-colored works of art.

The Modern Era

"We must always remember that the Lord sees us wrestling with the Enemy, and so we must never be afraid. Even should all hell fall upon us, we must be brave." – St. Silouan the Athonite

The monasteries on the peninsula struggled under the idiorrhythmic system and were beleaguered by mountains of debts between the 15th and 18th centuries. It wasn't until the early 19th century that the Athonites finally climbed out of the holes they had dug themselves. By 1820, most of the monasteries had paid off the bulk of their debts, and local authorities were also in the process of approving the construction of new monasteries, as well as much-needed renovations. As time progressed, more and more monasteries returned to the age-old cenobitic way of life.

Unfortunately, political chaos around the peninsula would strike again shortly after. On the 21st of February in 1821, the Greek War of Independence brought about a spate of Turkish attacks on the Holy Mountain. The peninsula was soon captured by the Ottoman forces, who proceeded to establish a temporary headquarters in Athos, as well as garrisons in several monasteries. The eight-year war was finally concluded in February 1830 with the London Protocol, which officially recognized Greece as an "independent, sovereign state." The last of the Ottomans were only ousted from the mainland in 1912.

For the next 14 years, international councils vigorously deliberated over the peninsula's fate. The first round of discourse was settled with the 1926 Treaty of Lausanne, which placed Athos within the dominion of Greek monarchs, or more specifically, a "self-governing part of the Greek state," thus creating the "Monastic State of Hagion Oros."

For a fleeting moment, peace prevailed, but in 1941, mere months after the Nazis poured into Greece, Mount Athos found itself at the center of a dilemma like no other. In the summer of that fateful year, Professor Franz Dölger arrived at the peninsula and proceeded to carry out a Nazi-themed expedition. Alfred Rosenberg, Reich Minister for the Occupied Eastern Territories, is said to have funded the expedition.

Rosenberg

Dölger's entourage, composed of a mix of intellectuals and military officers, was fully prepared to seize the peninsula by force if necessary, but much to their astonishment, the Athonites appeared to be far more well-disposed to the Germans' unannounced visit. As a matter of fact, they welcomed them with open arms, with a few elders even lauding Hitler as a "great German king who slays the Bolsheviks and the Jews," which they called a "fulfillment of prophecy." Some say the Athonites had no choice but to dance to the tune of the Nazis' fiddle, not to escape what would certainly be their grisly fates, but to ensure the safety of the peninsula's relics. Others claim that the isolated Athonites were unaware of the true depravity of Hitler's crimes. Scott Nevins, author of *The Hitler Icon: How Mount Athos Honored the Führer*, wrote, "In fairness to the residents of Mount Athos, we should note that they had good reason to despise Hitler's nemesis: Communism. Stalin was busy confiscating the Russian Orthodox Church's property and deporting its priests to the gulag, and he had also halted the previously reliable flow of Russian contributions to the monasteries' upkeep."

Whatever the case, the Athonites were keen to avoid the wrath of the Nazis, and the *Iera Espitasia* –a quartet of Athonite elders – took a page from their ancestors' book by penning a tactfully worded letter to the Führer himself. They kindly requested for the dictator to guarantee Mount Athos his personal protection, inflating his ego with the promise of the following title: High Protector of the Holy Mountain. Hitler agreed to this arrangement with great enthusiasm, and as a token of their gratitude, several Athonite monasteries mounted portraits of the dictator on their walls. Some monasteries were even accused of praying for him. Among the accused was the Saint Pantaleimon Monastery, which displayed their Hitler portrait directly below the framed photograph of the ousted Russian Tsar Nicholas II. As scandalized as those outside of the peninsula were about this admittedly serpentine tactic, it worked, because by the end of World War II, Mount Athos remained wholly intact. Conversely, those on the mainland lost 11% of their population, mainly its Jewish residents.

Today, visiting the exclusive peninsula is difficult, but not impossible. An estimated 110 entry visas are supposedly granted each day, consisting of 100 domestic visas and 10 international permits. On account of the number of applicants, pilgrims who wished to plan a trip to the peninsula must apply several months in advance, and owing to the absence of hotels and restaurants in Athos, pilgrims are also expected to book their living quarters with the monasteries themselves. The most commonly granted visa to this "territory within a territory" expire after four days.

Although children as young as 12 are now permitted on Athos (accompanied by an adult), the Byzantine era ban on women and female animals persists. Women have protested against this archaic law, but most have chosen, albeit grudgingly, to respect the prohibition. Other women have willingly trespassed on the property so notoriously off-limits to them, some sparked by defiance and others by the restless spirit of curiosity.

In fact, the first-ever "violation" of the female ban occurred in 1346. The trespasser was Jelen, queen consort of Serbian King Stefan Dušan, who came ashore uninvited. The queen was swiftly intercepted by vigilant monks before she could reach her intended destination, the Serbian Hilander Monastery.

An icon of Jesus in the Hilander Monastery

Mount Athos continued to periodically receive female visitors in the centuries that followed, but interest was inexplicably piqued in the early 1900s, which saw a sudden rash of celibacy-destroying trespassers. In 1929, 26-year-old Maryse Choisy, a disturbed French journalist, allegedly lopped off her own breasts, adopted a male disguise, and lugged her suitcases onto a rented ship, all for the precarious opportunity to experience life amongst the Athonite monks. There, Choisy reportedly remained for an entire month before her true gender was discovered. As soon as the "undercover" journalist returned home, she put pen to pad and documented her tantalizing experiences in a book entitled *A Month With the Men of Mount Athos.* Included in her incredible account were episodes involving a wildly "kinky," yet repentant monk.

Predictably, Choisy's book, branded as an exposé, went to the top of the charts almost at once, but Athonite elders dismissed her tale as no more than tawdry slander. "It is fanciful," reads the official statement released by the Athonites. "[Choisy] probably only saw Mount Athos from a boat. Further, how is it possible for a young and pretty girl, prone to adventures, to remain even a day in whatever type of outfit, amid 5,000 lively, stout monks, and not bring any of them...to temptation? [Could] she have remained unscathed for a month?"

Just three years after Choisy's alleged escapades on Mount Athos, 20-year-old beauty queen and polyglot Aliki Diplarakou, the first Greek contestant to be crowned "Miss Europe" in 1930, made an attempt of her own. As the story goes, Aliki stuffed her hair into her sailor's cap, donned a matching outfit, and crept onto the Athonite shore and into a monastery undetected. Rumor has it that the ravishing brunette caught the eye of a young, attractive monk. She apparently went as so far as to flirt with the unwitting brother, and even managed to snap a photograph of them together. When Aliki was eventually outed and her story was broadcasted by the media, the monk hung up his robes for the last time and left Athos for good. The smitten monk tracked her down with a ring in his pocket, only to discover that Aliki was already happily married. Devastated, the monk spiraled into a horrid depression and was ultimately driven mad by his heartbreak, spending the rest of his miserable days in a psychiatric facility.

The last straw would come in the spring of 1953. On the 17th of April, a 22-year-old woman named Maria Poimenidou adopted a male disguise and conned her way into a monastery, where she enjoyed the company of Athonite monks for two days. Understandably, Maria's visit prompted a furor on the peninsula, which led to the passing of "Legislative Decree 2623/1953." As stated by the decree, any woman who dared to set foot on Athos from that point forward would be subject to a maximum penalty of 12 months behind bars.

The only woman who has managed to obtain an invite was Eliza Charlotte Alexander, the second wife of Statford Canning, British ambassador to the Ottoman Empire, but even then, the Athonites made clear that such an invite was most likely a one-time phenomenon. As Patriarch Anthimos put it, the Athonites "understood the reasons for the visit, [but] he strictly recommended not repeating it."

Unyielding as the Athonites were about upholding the ban on women, they were known to show compassion to their neighbors during dire times. Mount Athos served as a hideout for women and children refugees twice, once in the Greek War of Independence, and again during the three-year Greek Civil War of 1946.

The peninsula's prohibition on women is just one of the controversies clinging to the Athonites' reputation. An article from the April 1941 issue of *Time Magazine* highlighted some of the other supposed debauchery that the Athonites engaged in. "[An] alarming number of [Athonite] monks have taken to smoking, alcohol, [and] even narcotics," the article exclaimed. "And the immemorial escape from celibacy has threatened to become a fever sickening the whole 'Great Academy of the Greek Clergy.' The Greek press has stormed about the kidnapping of male children for the monks of Athos, and motorboats carrying male prostitutes are constantly reported chugging into the monastery harbors."

Athonites have also been maligned by critics for their views on certain human rights issues, especially within the LGBT community. In a shocking interview entitled "They Take Psychotropic Drugs on Mount Athos," published by the "E" (Εψιλον) magazine in April 2001, a former Athonite monk by the name of Michael Haztiantoniou vilified the monks for a number of hypocrisies, including their treatment of homosexual monks. According to Brother Michael, who lived on Athos between 1973 and 1988, an Athonite monk from a nearby monastery suddenly died of an unspecified illness. When authorities discovered that the deceased was gay, they immediately decided to wash their hands clean of him, refusing him the honor of burying him alongside his fellow monks. His name was also omitted from the *Kuvaras*.

The Athonites have also been criticized for their active campaign against transgender individuals in recent years, branding it "gender dysphoria" and a Satan-given "mental illness." This was their response to a 2017 law that enabled Greek citizens over the age of 15 to alter the genders on their national identity cards without proof of a sex-change operation: "It is another violation of God's law, just like existing legislation which permits cohabitation agreements between same-sex couples. If we do not resist, then our ancestors will rise from their graves." In the same breath, they argued that transgender men, whom they regarded as "women," could now visit Mount Athos as they pleased without suffering any legal repercussions.

Today, many blame the irresistibly seductive powers of 21st century technology, amongst other factors, for the dramatic decrease in the peninsula's population. In 1905, official records indicate that there were 7,553 monks on Mount Athos, and the ethnicities of the Athonite residents were "3,207 Greeks, 3,615 Russians, 340 Bulgarians, 288 Romanians, 53 Georgians, 18 Servians, and 32 belonging to other nationalities." There were 21 principal monasteries, listed according to their place on the hierarchy: "The Great Lavra, Iviron, Vatopedi, Chilandarion, St. Dionysus, Coutloumousi, Pantocrator, Xiropatamos, Zograf, Docheiarion, Caracalla, Philotheos, Simopetra, St. Paul, Stauroniceta, Xenophon, Osiou Gregoriou, Esphigmenon, St. Panteleimon, St. Anna, and finally the Monastery of Karyses."

Recently, the first road was built on Mount Athos, courtesy of Greek authorities, but such things could do nothing to heal the deteriorating morale and increasing differences widening the rift between the Athonite brothers. The once-coveted peninsula's loss in appeal was undeniable, as the 40,000 monks who once lived there during its height in the 1300s had dwindled away to 7,500 by the 20th century. Numbers continued to plunge, and today, only about 1,500 monks remain.

Online Resources

Other books about Greece by Charles River Editors

Other books about Mount Athos on Amazon

Bibliography

Editors, B. *Why Are Women Banned from Mount Athos?* 27 May 2016, www.bbc.com/news/magazine-36378690. Accessed 4 July 2018.

Editors, S L. *The Land and Its People.* 2015, sacredland.org/mount-athos-greece/. Accessed 4 July 2018.

Editors, V M. *Mount Athos Chronology.* 2015, www.visitmountathos.eu/chronology.html. Accessed 4 July 2018.

Editors, M H. *The History of Mount Athos.* 2017, www.macedonian-heritage.gr/Athos/General/History.html. Accessed 4 July 2018.

Editors, S D. *Mount Athos, Greece.* 2013, www.sacred-destinations.com/greece/mt-athos. Accessed 4 July 2018.

Editors, O. *Facts about Mount Athos You Should Know.* 21 June 2018, ouranoupoli.gr/facts-about-mount-athos-you-should-know/. Accessed 4 July 2018.

Nevins, S. *A Short History of Women Who Have Entered Mount Athos [Updated].* 31 Jan. 2015, scottnevinssuicide.wordpress.com/2015/01/31/a-short-history-of-women-who-have-entered-mount-athos/. Accessed 4 July 2018.

Sanidopoulos, J. *Women Who Violated the Avaton of Mount Athos.* 4 Aug. 2014, www.johnsanidopoulos.com/2014/08/women-who-violated-avaton-of-mount-athos.html. Accessed 4 July 2018.

Squires, N. *Monks of Mt Athos Fear New Gender Law Could Enable Women into Their All-Male Sanctuary.* 17 Oct. 2017, www.telegraph.co.uk/news/2017/10/17/monks-mt-athos-fear-new-gender-law-could-enable-women-all-male/. Accessed 4 July 2018.

Grohmann, K. *Greek Women Enter Male-Only Mount Athos Community.* 9 Jan. 2008, www.reuters.com/article/us-greece-women-athos/greek-women-enter-male-only-mount-athos-community-idUSL0945881020080109. Accessed 4 July 2018.

Nevins, S. *The Hitler Icon: How Mount Athos Honored the Führer.* 21 Feb. 2016, scottnevinssuicide.wordpress.com/2016/02/21/the-hitler-icon-how-mount-athos-honored-the-fuhrer/. Accessed 4 July 2018.

Nevins, S. *Mount Athos, Homosexuality, Addiction to Heavy Psychotropic Drugs & Suicide (Monk Michael, 2001).* 26 Jan. 2016, scottnevinssuicide.wordpress.com/2016/01/26/mount-athos-homosexuality-addiction-to-heavy-psychotropic-drugs-έψιλον-τεύχος-524/. Accessed 4 July 2018.

Editors, O C. *26 Martyrs of the Zographou Monastery on Mt. Athos at the Hands of the Crusaders*. 10 Oct. 2013, oca.org/saints/lives/2013/10/10/108024-26-martyrs-of-the-zographou-monastery-on-mt-athos-at-the-hands-o. Accessed 4 July 2018.

Orthodox Christian Quotes. Edited by S Mojsovki and K Wilkerson, 1 Nov. 2007, theodorakis.net/orthodoxquotescomplete.html. Accessed 4 July 2018.

Findler, R, and M Fidler. *The Holy Mountain: Monks of Mount Athos – Photo Essay*. 5 Jan. 2017, www.theguardian.com/artanddesign/2017/jan/05/the-holy-mountain-monks-of-mount-athos-photo-essay. Accessed 4 July 2018.

Gray, M. *Mount Athos*. 2017, sacredsites.com/europe/greece/mount_athos.html. Accessed 4 July 2018.

Editors, M. *A History of Mount Athos*. 2017, www.monachos.net/library/index.php/monasticism/athos/113-a-history-of-mount-athos. Accessed 4 July 2018.

Editors, C P. *The History Of Mount Athos*. 2018, www.christian-pilgrimage-journeys.com/mount-athos/history-mount-athos/. Accessed 4 July 2018.

Editors, C P. *The History Of Mount Athos (4th Century - 14th Century)*. 2017, www.christian-pilgrimage-journeys.com/mount-athos/4thcentury-14thcentury/. Accessed 4 July 2018.

Dilouambaka, E. *A Brief History Of Mount Athos*. 28 Oct. 2016, theculturetrip.com/europe/greece/articles/a-brief-history-of-mount-athos/. Accessed 4 July 2018.

Roten, J G. *Mount Athos and Mary*. 2017, udayton.edu/imri/mary/m/mount-athos-and-mary.php. Accessed 5 July 2018.

Editors, O C. *No Girls Allowed – The Greek State That Forbids Both Human and Animal Females*. 23 Jan. 2015, www.odditycentral.com/travel/no-girls-allowed-the-greek-state-that-forbids-both-human-and-animal-females.html. Accessed 5 July 2018.

Editors, V. *Mount Athos in Greece Forbids Women from Entering Because of a Religious Reason (11 Pics)*. 23 June 2016, www.vorply.com/world/list/find-out-why-mount-athos-in-greece-is-forbidden-for-women/. Accessed 5 July 2018.

Foster, D. *One Small Step for Womankind in an All-Male Greek State*. 18 Sept. 2012, www.theguardian.com/commentisfree/belief/2012/sep/18/mount-athos-male-greek-state. Accessed 5 July 2018.

Editors, H C. *BYZANTINE EMPIRE*. 2017, www.history.com/topics/ancient-history/byzantine-empire. Accessed 5 July 2018.

Editors, A. *Byzantine Empire*. 28 Apr. 2011, www.ancient.eu/Byzantine_Empire/. Accessed 5 July 2018.

Editors, C N. *Mt. Athos: A Visit to the Holy Mountain*. 22 May 2011, www.cbsnews.com/news/mt-athos-a-visit-to-the-holy-mountain/. Accessed 5 July 2018.

Draper, R. *Called to the Holy Mountain*. Dec. 2009, www.nationalgeographic.com/magazine/2009/12/athos/. Accessed 5 July 2018.

Editors, M H. *THE MONKS OF MOUNT ATHOS*. 2018, www.marbleheadsalt.com/the-monks/. Accessed 5 July 2018.

Editors, O W. *Seventh Ecumenical Council*. 27 Nov. 2012, orthodoxwiki.org/Seventh_Ecumenical_Council. Accessed 5 July 2018.

Editors, N W. *Second Council of Nicaea*. 26 Aug. 2015, www.newworldencyclopedia.org/entry/Second_Council_of_Nicaea. Accessed 5 July 2018.

Editors, R. *Battle of Thasos* . 5 May 2018, www.revolvy.com/main/index.php?s=Battle of Thasos. Accessed 5 July 2018.

Kalimniou, D. *The Battle for Arabic Crete*. 25 May 2018, neoskosmos.com/en/116044/the-battle-for-arabic-crete/. Accessed 5 July 2018.

Hendrix, D. *Monasteries of Mount Athos*. 2016, www.thebyzantinelegacy.com/athos. Accessed 5 July 2018.

Editors, V M. *History*. 2015, www.visitmountathos.eu/history.html. Accessed 5 July 2018.

Economidis, N. *The History of Mount Athos During the Byzantine Age*. 2017, www.elpenor.org/athos/en/e21811.asp. Accessed 5 July 2018.

Cartwright, M. *Mount Athos*. 18 Apr. 2018, www.ancient.eu/Mount_Athos/. Accessed 5 July 2018.

Editors, M A. *Athos, Geography and History*. 2013, en.mountathosarea.org/our-area/mount-athos/. Accessed 5 July 2018.

Hendrix, D. *Monastery of the Great Lavra*. 2016, www.thebyzantinelegacy.com/lavra-athos. Accessed 5 July 2018.

Editors, P U. *Rules, Chrysobulls and the Wine Trade on Athos*. 17 Aug. 2014, pemptousia.com/2014/08/rules-chrysobulls-and-the-wine-trade-on-athos/. Accessed 5 July 2018.

Editors, M H. *The Monastery of Megisti Lavra*. 2016, www.macedonian-heritage.gr/Athos/Monastery/Megisti Lavra.html. Accessed 6 July 2018.

Editors, M. *Mount Athos Great Lavra*. 2017, www.monastiria.gr/mount-athos/mount-athos-great-lavra-2/?lang=en. Accessed 6 July 2018.

Posner, D L. *Mount Athos*. Apr. 1964, www.poetryfoundation.org/poetrymagazine/browse?contentId=29716. Accessed 6 July 2018.

Editors, V H. *Mount Athos*. 2018, www.visit-halkidiki.gr/mount-athos/. Accessed 6 July 2018.

Editors, G B. *The "Three Fingers" of the Halkidiki Peninsula*. 2017, www.greekboston.com/travel/halkidiki-peninsula/. Accessed 6 July 2018.

Sanidopoulos, J. *Are Female Animals Forbidden On Mount Athos?* 16 Jan. 2016, www.johnsanidopoulos.com/2016/01/are-female-animals-forbidden-in-mount.html. Accessed 6 July 2018.

Editors, G M. *Apollo*. 2015, www.greekmythology.com/Olympians/Apollo/apollo.html. Accessed 6 July 2018.

Editors, G G. *Apollo and Daphne*. 30 Nov. 2016, greekgodsandgoddesses.net/myths/apollo-and-daphne/. Accessed 6 July 2018.

Sanidopoulos, J. *Alexander the Great, Mount Athos, & a Lofty Proposal*. 30 Apr. 2012, www.johnsanidopoulos.com/2012/04/alexander-great-mount-athos-and-lofty.html. Accessed 6 July 2018.

Editors, O W. *Marcian*. 24 Oct. 2012, orthodoxwiki.org/Marcian. Accessed 6 July 2018.

Džalto, D. *Iconoclastic Controversies*. 2015, www.khanacademy.org/humanities/medieval-world/byzantine1/beginners-guide-byzantine/a/iconoclastic-controversies. Accessed 6 July 2018.

Beşliu, P. *The Archaeology of the Medieval Towers in Mount Athos. An Attempt of Archaeological Research*. 28 Jan. 2011, revistatransilvania.ro/wp-content/uploads/2018/02/12.Muntean.pdf. Accessed 6 July 2018.

Editors, O W. *Canon (Hymn)*. 12 Aug. 2009, orthodoxwiki.org/Canon_(hymn). Accessed 6 July 2018.

Appleton, R. *Mount Athos*. 2007, www.newadvent.org/cathen/02047b.htm. Accessed 6 July 2018.

Editors, R. *Protos (Monastic Office)* . 31 Jan. 2018, www.revolvy.com/topic/Protos-(monastic-office). Accessed 6 July 2018.

Editors, E B. *Saint Athanasius the Athonite*. 17 Apr. 2015, www.britannica.com/biography/Saint-Athanasius-the-Athonite. Accessed 6 July 2018.

Editors, O W. *Mount Athos*. 9 May 2016, orthodoxwiki.org/Mount_Athos. Accessed 6 July 2018.

Editors, O W. *Athanasius of Athos*. 22 Oct. 2012, orthodoxwiki.org/Athanasius_of_Athos. Accessed 9 July 2018.

Editors, D I. *A ROMANO-BYZANTINE INSTITUTE*. 2018, dialogos-institute.org/?byzantium. Accessed 9 July 2018.

Editors, R. *Second Council of Lyon*. 9 Mar. 2018, www.revolvy.com/main/index.php?s=Second Council of Lyon. Accessed 9 July 2018.

Editors, O W. *Zographou Monastery (Athos)*. 8 Jan. 2011, orthodoxwiki.org/Zographou_Monastery_(Athos). Accessed 9 July 2018.

Editors, E N. *'Not an Anthologist: John Bekkos as a Reader of the Fathers.'* 30 Oct. 2009, eirenikon.wordpress.com/2009/10/30/not-an-anthologist-john-bekkos-as-a-reader-of-the-fathers/. Accessed 9 July 2018.

Editors, R. *Gregory of Sinai* . 10 Jan. 2018, www.revolvy.com/main/index.php?s=Gregory of Sinai. Accessed 9 July 2018.

Editors, R. *Gregory Palamas*. 20 June 2018, www.revolvy.com/main/index.php?s=Gregory Palamas. Accessed 9 July 2018.

Editors, W S. *Catholic Encyclopedia (1913)/Mount Athos*. 6 Feb. 2012, en.wikisource.org/wiki/Catholic_Encyclopedia_(1913)/Mount_Athos. Accessed 9 July 2018.

Rentoulas, A. *Fasting and Feasting on Mount Athos*. 12 July 2016, www.greece-is.com/mt-athos-monastic-diet-food-soul/. Accessed 9 July 2018.

Editors, M H. *The Monastery of Konstamonitou*. 2017, www.macedonian-heritage.gr/Athos/Monastery/Konstamonitou.html. Accessed 9 July 2018.

Editors, P U. *The Holy Monastery of Koutloumousiou*. 5 Nov. 2011, pemptousia.com/2011/11/the-holy-monastery-of-koutloumousiou/. Accessed 9 July 2018.

Editors, M H. *The Monastery of Gregoriou*. 2017, www.macedonian-heritage.gr/Athos/Monastery/Gregoriou.html. Accessed 9 July 2018.

Editors, M. *Pantocrator Monastery*. 2017, www.monastiria.gr/mount-athos/mount-athos-pantocrators-monastery/?lang=en. Accessed 9 July 2018.

Hendrix, D. *Pantokrator Monastery*. 2016, www.thebyzantinelegacy.com/pantokrator-athos. Accessed 9 July 2018.

Editors, O W. *Council of Florence*. 7 Nov. 2011, orthodoxwiki.org/Council_of_Florence. Accessed 9 July 2018.

Liester, M B. *Hesychasm: A Christian Path of Transcendence*. 2000, www.theosophical.org/publications/1432. Accessed 9 July 2018.

Katz, N. *How Do Mount Athos Monks Stay so Healthy?* 8 Dec. 2011, www.cbsnews.com/news/how-do-mount-athos-monks-stay-so-healthy/. Accessed 9 July 2018.

Editors, V M. *Daily Life*. 2017, www.visitmountathos.eu/daily-life.html. Accessed 9 July 2018.

Tzimas, S. *A Monk Shares His Love of God, Food and Wine*. 7 Feb. 2016, www.ekathimerini.com/210035/article/ekathimerini/life/a-monk-shares-his-love-of-god-food-and-wine. Accessed 9 July 2018.

Ellis, J. *THE MYSTERIOUS MONKS OF MOUNT ATHOS*. 29 May 2016, www.jamesellisfitness.com/mysterious-monks-mount-athos/. Accessed 9 July 2018.

Editors, H M. *MONKS AND RITUALS OF DAILY LIFE*. 2017, holymountain.omeka.net/exhibits/show/holy-mountain/monks-and-rituals-of-daily-lif. Accessed 9 July 2018.

Editors, M. *Mount Athos Monastery of Gregoriou*. 2015, www.monastiria.gr/mount-athos/mount-athos-monastery-of-grigoriou/?lang=en. Accessed 9 July 2018.

Flynn, D. *Monastic Mount Athos Offers a Glimpse Back in Time*. 13 Nov. 2008, www.reuters.com/article/us-greece-athos/monastic-mount-athos-offers-a-glimpse-back-in-time-idUSTRE4AC3RY20081113. Accessed 9 July 2018.

Mantzaridis, G. *The Monastic Life: The Way of Perfection*. 27 Apr. 2015, pemptousia.com/2015/04/the-monastic-life-the-way-of-perfection-the-holy-mount-athos/. Accessed 9 July 2018.

Editors, V W. *Secrets of the World's Healthiest People: Mount Athos Monks – Part 1 Diet.* 12 Sept. 2015, vibrantliveswellbeing.com/the-worlds-healthiest-people-mount-athos-monks-part-1-diet/. Accessed 9 July 2018.

Editors, M A. *Mount Athos Sketes.* 2017, mountathos-eshop.com/en/mount-athos-true-guardian-greek-orthodoxy/mount-athos-sketes/. Accessed 9 July 2018.

Chrysochoidis, K. *Cells, Sketes, and Monasteries in Mt Athos' History.* 26 Feb. 2016, pemptousia.com/2016/02/32974/. Accessed 9 July 2018.

Editors, S R. *Traditional Skull Painting Practiced by the Monks on Mount Athos.* 8 Mar. 2014, strangeremains.com/2014/03/08/traditional-skull-painting-of-mt-athos-in-greece/. Accessed 9 July 2018.

Editors, C D. *The Burial Practices on Mt. Athos.* 28 Dec. 2017, blog.obitel-minsk.com/2017/12/the-burial-practices-on-mt-athos.html. Accessed 9 July 2018.

Editors, A O. *Hermitages of Karoulia.* 2018, www.atlasobscura.com/places/hermitages-of-karoulia. Accessed 9 July 2018.

Editors, M. *The Jesus Prayer.* 2015, www.monastiriaka.gr/en/the-jesus-prayer-n-92301.html. Accessed 9 July 2018.

Lockard, J. *Holy Misogyny.* 24 May 2011, souciant.com/2011/05/holy-misogyny/. Accessed 9 July 2018.

Chrysopoulos , P. *Aliki Diplarakou: Greece's First 'Miss Europe.'* 8 Feb. 2018, greece.greekreporter.com/2018/02/08/aliki-diplarakou-greeces-first-miss-europe/. Accessed 9 July 2018.

Romer, F. E. (Ed.). (1998). *Pomponius Mela's Description of the World.* University of Michigan Press.

Chupungco, A. J. (2016). *Handbook for Liturgical Studies, Volume V: Liturgical Time and Space*(Vol. V). Liturgical Press.

Herrin, J. (2008). *Byzantium: The Surprising Life of a Medieval Empire.* Penguin UK.

Bryer, A., & Cunningham, M. (2016). *Mount Athos and Byzantine Monasticism: Papers from the Twenty-Eighth Spring Symposium of Byzantine Studies, University of Birmingham.* Routledge.

Free Books by Charles River Editors

We have brand new titles available for free most days of the week. To see which of our titles are currently free, click on this link.

Discounted Books by Charles River Editors

We have titles at a discount price of just 99 cents everyday. To see which of our titles are currently 99 cents, click on this link.

Made in the USA
Columbia, SC
18 April 2019